DATE DUE

First published in October 1992.
Created and produced for Ediciones B, S.A.
by o3 BCN Packagers.
Text: Albert Delmar
Translation: A. Lopes
Illustrations: F. Salvà

Rocafort, 104 08015 Barcelona (Spain)

ISBN: 84 - 406 - 3122 - 7
Depósito legal: CO 1027 - 1992
Printed and bound in Spain

Cover:
Self-portrait (1640)
Oil on canvas, 43.8x31.6 inches
National Gallery, London.

U.S. & Canada Sole Importer/ Distributor
Trans-National Trade Development Corporation
New York City
Toll Free: (800) 592-2209
Telephone: (212) 922-0450
Fax: (212) 922-0462

Printed by Graficromo, S.A.
Córdoba (Spain)

REMBRANDT

Merchand of Amsterdam

The story of Rembrandt

Rembrandt Harmensz van Rijn, the ninth child of a malt miller named Harmen Gerritsz van Rijn, was born in Leiden, a prosperous city in Holland, in 1606.

At that time, Holland was fighting for its independence from Spain. With its powerful fleet of some six thousand ships, it was becoming the world's major commercial power.

Rembrandt, Rubens, Frans Hals, Van Goyen, Steen, Ruysdael, Vermeer and other important painters all lived in Holland at almost the same time. It was the golden age of Dutch painting.

At the age of seven, little Rembrandt attended Latin School, and seven years later he attended a university in the city of his birth.

We do not know what subjects he studied at school or at the university, nor whether he was a good student or not. Actually, we know very little about Rembrandt's life. Most of what has been written about him is supposed.

What they taught him at the university did not interest him very much, and soon he chose a trade to earn his living - he decided to become a painter. He had showed a great talent for drawing and his mind was made up. His parents consented immediately.

Rembrandt began an apprenticeship at the studio of the painter Swanenburgh, who must have been a good teacher, because the boy made great progress during the three years that he was there.

Once he had finished his appenticeship, Rembrandt left for Amsterdam with his friend Jan Lievens. There they frequented the studio of the painter Pieter Lastman for six months. A receipt witten by the master has been saved to this day:"Received from Harmen, son of Gerritz of Leiden, the quantity of two florins fifty for having taught painting during a half year to Rembrandt, son of Harmen".

Shortly thereafter, back in Leiden, Rembrandt set up his first studio with his friend Jan Lieves.

They worked as a team, and there are even some paintings signed by both of them. But soon Rembrandt's greater talent became clear.

His work was very successful right from the beginning, and he was immediately considered a great master.

Even then, in a book about the city of Leiden, someone wrote

"...and his hand was so fortunate that he became one of the most celebrated painters of our century".

More proof of his success is that at the age of 22, Rembrandt already had his first pupil.

Doctor Tulp's anatomy lesson

Rembrandt painted this at the age of 26, in Amsterdam. He acheived great success with it.

He had just moved to that city, precisely in the hope of obtaining important assignments such as this painting.

It represents a group of members of the Surgeons Guild of Amsterdam attending a conference demonstrated by an important colleague.

Doctor Tulp's anatomy lesson (1632)
Oil on canvas, 65x86.6 inches
Mauritshuis, The Hague.

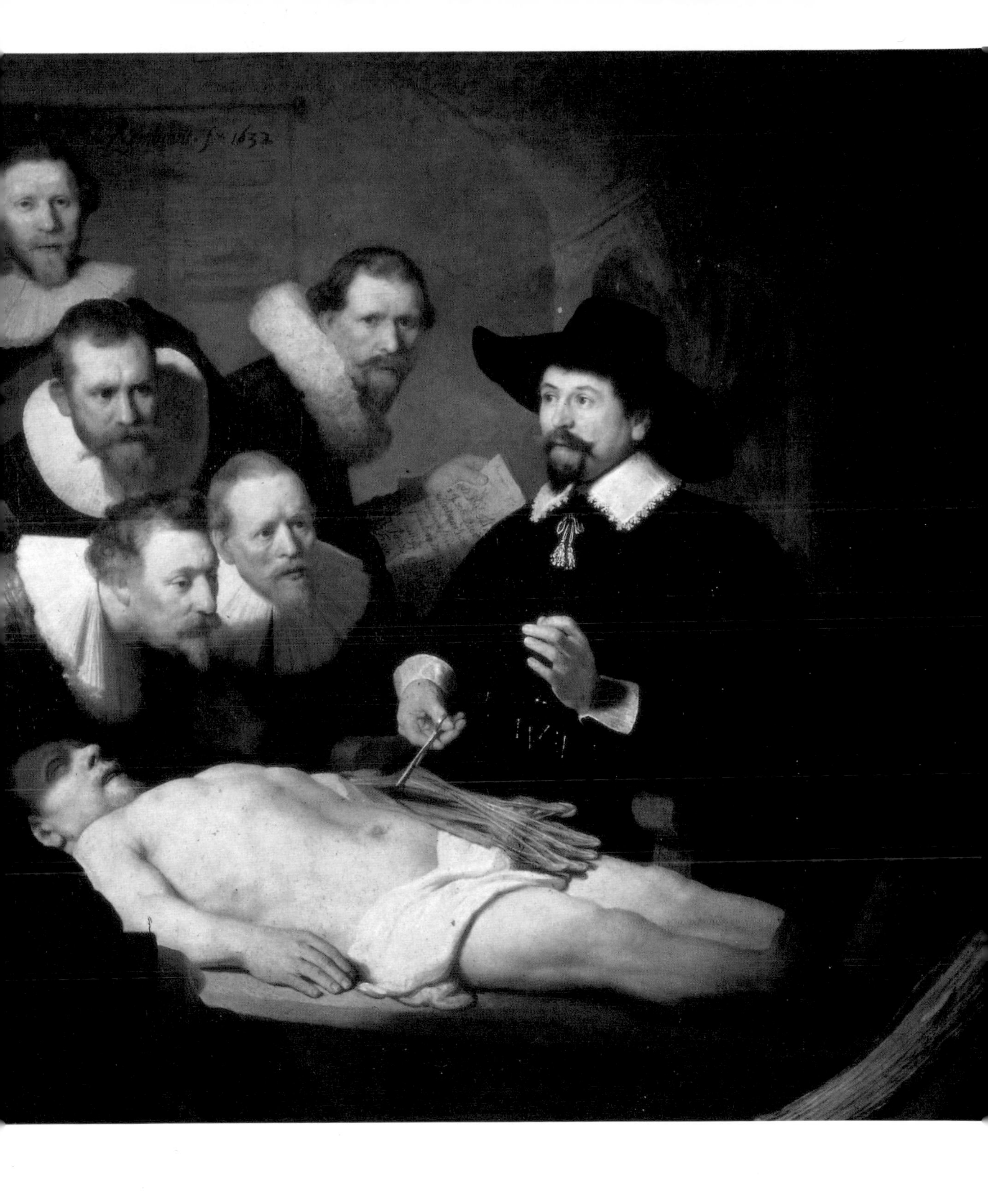

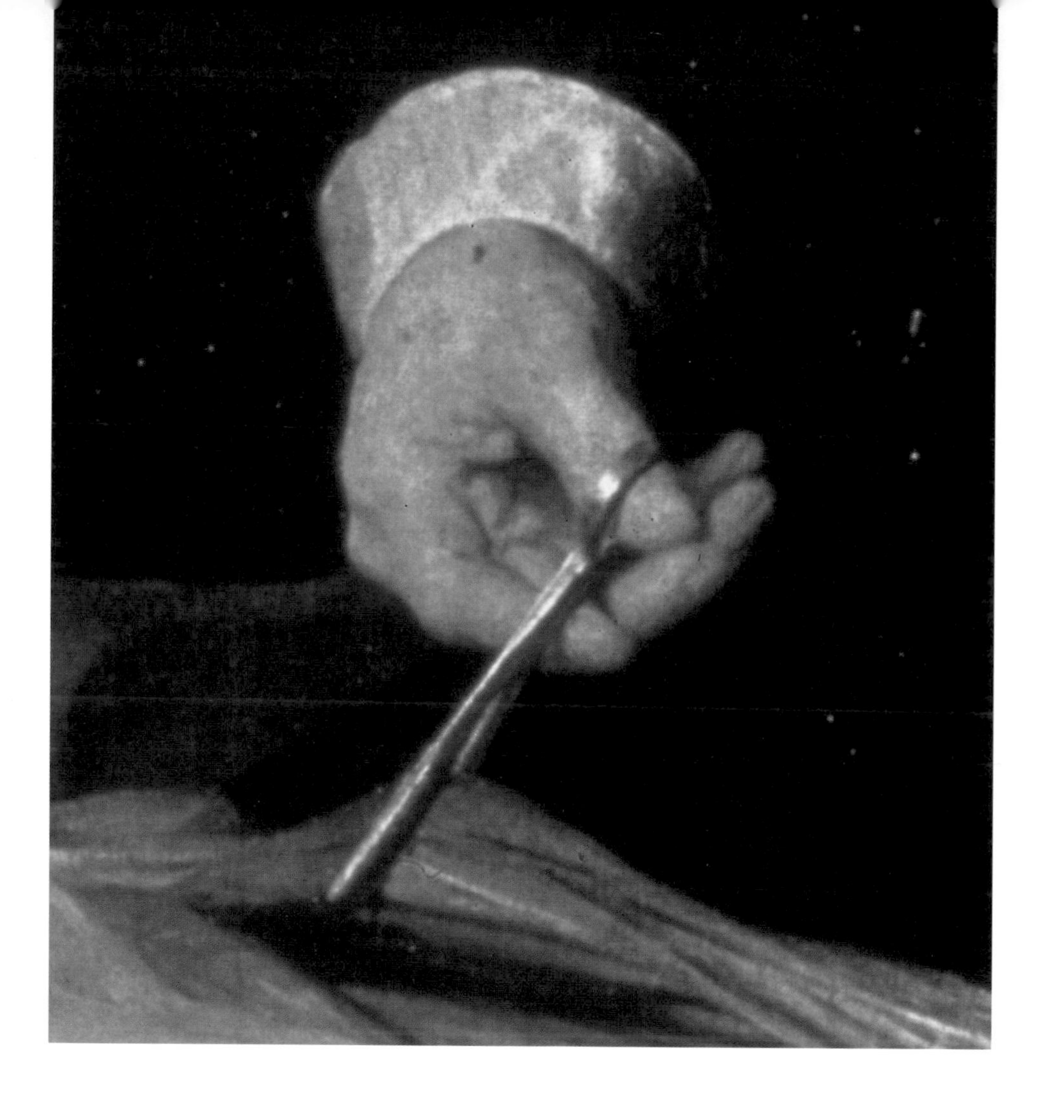

The dissection of a human body was not something that happened very frequently.

Rembrandt attended the session and managed to create a special atmosphere for this rare event. The lecturer's black suit contrasts with the sheen of the corpse and of his own hands.

It is interesting to note how each of the attendants listens to the lecture in a different way.

The people who are behind the corpse, leaning forward, listen with great interest and pay attention to everything that Doctor Tulp is doing.

The doctors who are more to the left are not paying as much attention to the lecturer. One of them is listening to what the doctor is saying but the other seems to be a bit distracted and is looking out of the picture.

The seven figures are distributed in a triangle. At the top, one of the attendants looks at us and points to something. Another is holding a paper with the names of everyone attending the conference written on it.

Night round

This large picture is one of Rembrandt's masterpieces, painted at the age of 36.

Once it was finished, the people portrayed were not satisfied with the results because some of them considered that their portrait did not stand out enough in the composition. This conflict might be one the of the reasons why Rembrandt began to lose popularity in Amsterdam.

Night round (1642)
Oil on canvas, 154.8x200.8 inches
Risksmuseum, Amsterdam.

Despite its title, this canvas actually represents a group of people who belong to the Marksmen's Society of Amsterdam, leaving for a parade or a shooting competition, led by captain Frans Banning Cocq.

It is the moment when the drum calls the company to line up. The guns are readied, there is a sense of expectation and certain commotion. A gun is shot and a dog barks. Some children run among the members of the company.

These people are not posing quietly. The lively sense of movement that Rembrandt achieves was something totally new in these types of portraits.

The man with the red sash in the center is captain Cocq. On his left is deputy Willem van Ruytenburch, his lieutenant, dressed in yellow.

Self-portrait

Rembrandt painted this picture during the last year of his life, at the age of 63.

Of the six hundred pictures that Rembrandt painted, four hundred are portraits. Some of them were assignments that he did to earn a living, but a good number of them he did on his own, because they interested him. He painted portraits of his parents, of his wife, of his son Titus, of his neighbors... This allowed him to work with more freedom, without having to give in to the whims of clients.

At that time, Rembrandt was criticized for painting portraits not only of the most important persons of the city, but also of old people, sick people and destitute people, which was not considered to be in very good taste.

Self-portrait (1669)
Oil on canvas, 23.6x20.4 inches
Mauritshuis, The Hague.

Rembrandt painted more than sixty self-portraits - one of every ten of his works. Through them, we can learn a lot about the painter - what he looked like at different stages of his life, how he felt...

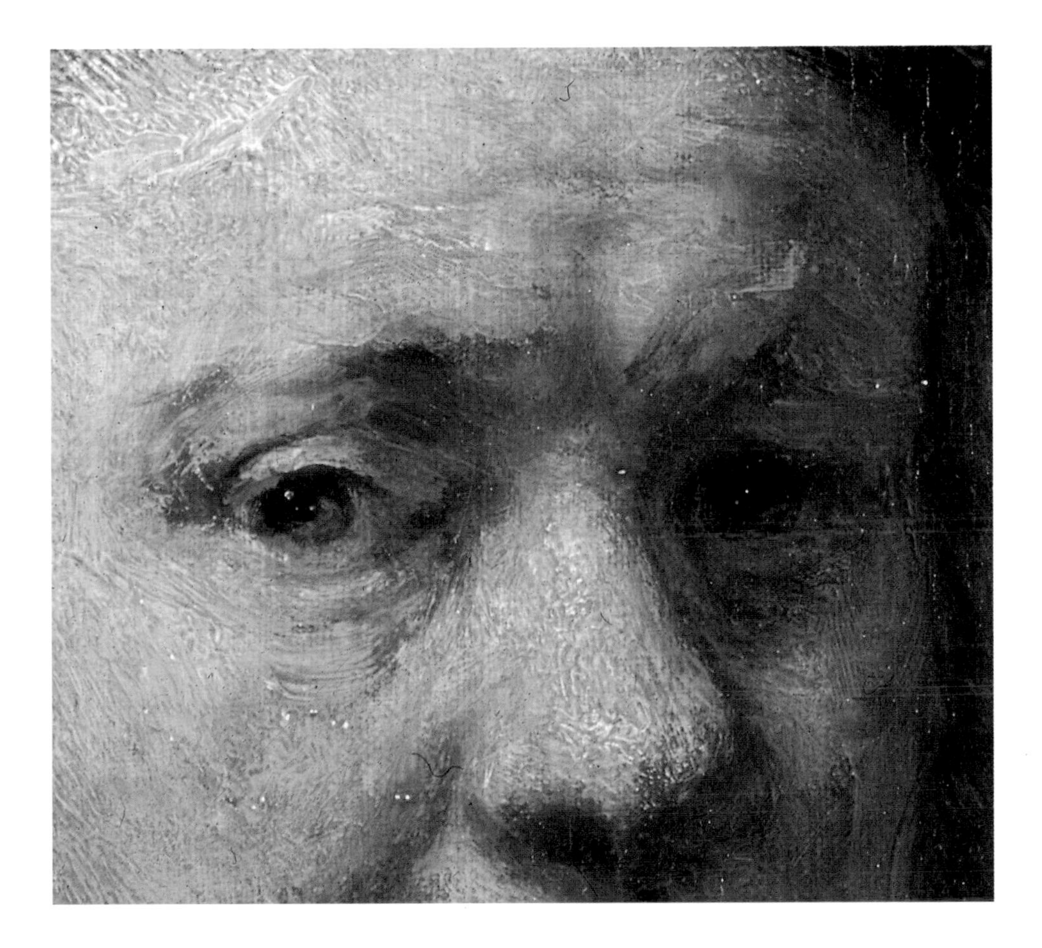

Here Rembrandt represents himself as tired and old. It seems that he needed to study himself well in order to portray the faces of other people and reflect their personalities.

Amsterdam, thanks to its port, was one of the most important cities in the world. People of all races and from all places roamed its streets.

Government workers, bankers, merchants, industrialists, rich craftsmen... they all wanted portraits of themselves and of their families. There was a lot of work for a painter. After his father died and Rembrandt had received his share of the inheritance, he moved into the house of the art dealer Hendrich van Uylenburgh in the search of money and the assignments the rich habitants of the city could provide him with.

In Amsterdam, Rembrandt's fame grew rapidly. In light of so much interest, he could ask high prices for his paintings. In his studio he had some pupils who, in addition to helping him, also paid him a good price for their apprenticeship with him.

When he was 28 he married Saskia, his art dealer's niece. She was young and beautiful and belonged to a family of more position and wealth than his.

During the following years of his marriage, Rembrandt continued to enjoy great success. He earned lots of money, but spent even more, without worrying about saving or investing his earnings.

After the death of his wife Saskia, everything in Rembrandt's life began to change. Due to the debts that he had accumulated, his estate was auctioned, and he was left with nothing. He was forced to move and live a much simpler life, without the comforts he had grown accustomed to.

Because of this, his style of painting evolved - more and more personal and out of fashion - which was no longer to the liking of the bourgeois of Amsterdam. He continued to get work, but the assignments came in less and less frequently.

Self-portrait (1634)
Oil on canvas, 26.8x21.6 inches
Galeria Uffizi, Florence.

Artemisa (1634)
Oil on canvas, 56.8x61.2 inches
Museo del Prado, Madrid.

The lawer (1634)
Oil on canvas, 56.4x54 inches
National Gallery, Prague.

Rembrandt Van Rijn

1606 Born on July 15th in Leiden, Holland.

1613-20 He attends Latin School.

1621-23 He works as apprentice to the painter Jacob van Swanenburgh.

1624 He goes to Amsterdam, where he frequents the studio of the painter Pieter Lastman.

1625 He returns to Leiden, and sets up as an independent painter.

1626 He paints *Tobías and Ann with baby goat* and *Balaam's mule.*

1629 He paints *Judas repentant returning the silver coins to the High Priests.*

1630 His father dies in April.

1631 He moves to Amsterdam. He paints his first well-known painting: *Nicolaes Ruts.*

1632 On assignment, he paints *Dr. Tulp's anatomy lesson.* He achieves great reknown as a portraitist.

1633 He paints *Descending from the Cross.*

1634 On June 22hd he marries Saskia Uylenburgh. He becomes a member of the Corporation of Saint Lucas. He paints *The happy couple* and *Artemisa.*

1635 His first son Robertus is born.

1636 He paints *Landscape with stone door, The blinding of Samson* and *Delilah.*

1638 His daughter Cornelia is born, but dies shortly thereafter.

1640 In July his second daughter Cornelia is born, but only lives a few weeks. In September his mother dies.

Portrait of an 83 - year - old woman (1634)
Oil on wood, 27.48x21.52 inches
National Gallery, London.

Allegory of the vine workers (1637)
Oil on wood, 12.4x16.8 inches
Hermitage Museum, St. Petersburg.

The skinned ox (1655)
Oil on wood, 37.6x26.8 inches
Museé du Louvre, Paris.

1641 His son Titus is born - of Rembrandt and Saskia's four children, the only one who did not die prematurely. He begins *Night Round*, which he finishes the following year.

1642 His wife Saskia dies in June. Geertje Dircks comes to the house to take care of Titus.

1646-47-48 He paints *The Adoration of the shepherds, Susan and the old men* and *Christ in Emaús*.

1649 Because of problems with Geertje Dircks, Rembrandt is involved in a legal process for breach of matrimomy.

1653 He paints *Aristóteles*.

1654 He paints *Woman bathing*. In October his daughter Cornelia is born, fruit of an extramarital affair with Hendrickje Stoffels.

1656-58 Rembrandt's paintings, drawings, engravings, art collection, possessions and house are sold at auction.

1662 He paints *The draper's union* and *The Batavian conspiracy led by Claudio Civile*

1663 Hendrickje Stoffels dies.

1665 He paints *The Jewish bride*.

1669 He paints his last self-portrait, and dies on October 4th at the age of 63.

Rembrandt's works are principally located in:
Museum of Fine Arts, Boston, Massachusetts, U.S.A
National Gallery, London, England.
Musée du Louvre, Paris, France.
National Gallery, Washington, D.C., U.S.A.
Metropolitan Museum of Art, New York, New York, U.S.A.